THE LITTLE GUIDE TO GREATER GLORY AND A HAPPIER LIFE

THE LITTLE GUIDE TO GREATER GLORY AND A HAPPIER LIFE

By

Sri M

Magenta Press

Second Edition 2010.
Third Edition 2014.
Reprint 2020.

ISBN: 978-81-956089-8-0

2022 Edition

Book Design: J. Menon. www.grantha.com

Printed at Thomson Press India Ltd

Published by Magenta Press & Publication Pvt. Ltd.
No. 1st Floor,Webster Road, Cox Town,
Bengaluru - 560005. Karnataka, India
Tel: +91 93430 715 37 / +91 63630 835 90
info@magentapress.in / www.magentapress.in

My Param Guru Sri Guru Babaji.

My Guru Sri Maheshwaranath Babaji.

CONTENTS

A PROFILE OF 'M'

The boy was just eight years old when he saw the strange being. He was the son of a deccani Muslim family, settled in Trivandrum, the beautiful capital of Kerala. Having heard stories of angels coming down to bless Mohammed and other prophets and saints from his devout grandmother, he thought at first that it was an angel. He was frightened.

Standing under the big jackfruit tree behind the house was an effulgent figure. The boy was rooted to the spot. The figure approached. It was not an angel.

The man in a single white loin-cloth, with long hair and sparse beard touched the boy on his shoulders and said in Deccani, "I am your teacher. You will not meet me for many years after this, but you will have to finish the studies that you left incomplete. You will not be allowed to tell anyone about me until the time is ripe." With that he walked away.

That was the first initiation. Two years later, while playing hide and seek, the boy experienced what may be described in yogic terms as Keval Kumbhak – the suspension of inhalation and exhalation. Bliss filled his heart. The breathing resumed in a few minutes.

Soon he could get into it at will with a deep sigh. The bliss that he experienced convinced him that a greater world existed within his being – a world of spiritual bliss.

To all outward appearance he was just like any other boy except that he loved religious scriptures and philosophy – no matter of which religion, devotional songs and discussions on God, saints and sages.

When he was ten, he used to go in the evenings to a certain house which belonged to Mr. Pillai, whose nephew and son-in-law tutored him in mathematics. One evening he entered Pillai's house as usual and found himself face to face with a venerable, sturdy man of about sixty years, clean shaven and with closely cropped silver grey hair, wearing a half sleeved shirt and loin cloth, sitting cross-legged on a bench. The room smelled of incense.

"Hello!" said the old man in Malayalam, "Come, come. Don't be afraid."

'M' walked up to him. The man patted his back and caressed his neck and head and said, "Umm. Good! Everything will be all right in good time."

Again the breathless condition and greater bliss. 'M' stood up and went straight home. The guidance had begun. He was the first of the great souls 'M' was to meet in the course of his spiritual journey.

Much later 'M' came to know that the man was a great selfrealised soul who lived in Atma Bhava and was simply called Pujapura Swami since he lived in Pujapura. He was unmarried but not a formal monk. In his youth he had been initiated into yogic practices by a great teacher and ever since had lived a model life, his heart absorbed in the blissful, Supreme Brahman while he performed his duties like an ordinary mortal.

'M' also learnt that the Swami used to hold midnight Satsangs on certain days, which a great sanyasin, who had renounced even his loin-cloth, would sometimes attend. Pujapura Swami was not known outside a small circle because he forbade propaganda.

When 'M' was seventeen, the sanyasin was no more, but a friend handed over a compilation of his teaching to 'M' which was privately circulated. It contained the essence of Vedanta in very simple language.

By then, the knowledge that 'M' needed from time to time as he progressed on the path began to come to him automatically. His father borrowed B. K. S. Iyengar's "Light on Yoga" from a friend of his (his father was never an orthodox Muslim). 'M' read it through. A yoga teacher, Sri Sharma, gave him his initial lessons on Yogasanas and Surya Namaskaras.

'M' met Swami Tapasyananda of the Ramakrishna Mission, a direct disciple of Sarada Devi. He was then the head of Ramakrishna Mission at Trivandrum. The librarian at the Trivandrum Public Library kept 'M' well supplied with the works of Vivekananda. He chanced to read Swami Chinmayananda's Japa Yoga and Gayatri and he began to chant the Gayatri Mantra. A Tantric instructed him in certain mantras and lent him Arthur Avalon's "Serpent Power." He read many other books – the Upanishads, the Gita, Yogic texts and Vedanta included. He discovered that Sanskrit was not too difficult to understand.

Side by side with gaining theoretical knowledge, he meditated for long hours, especially at midnight. He had merely to shut his eyes and concentrate on the lotus of the heart to enter into Keval Kumbhak and experience tremendous bliss and extraordinary vision of divine lights and voices. Sometimes terrifying visions would flit across his mind but they would pass and he would once again be filled with ecstasy.

Then he met a great person known as Chempazanthi Swami. The Jesuits had started their first Loyola Junior College at Sreekaryam in Trivandrum and 'M' was among the first batch of pre-degree students. A few kilometers away was the remote village of Chempazanthi which is the birth place of Sri Narayana Guru, the great reformer-saint. Close to Chempazanthi is Chenkotkonam where the Swami lived.

He was a tea-shop owner turned saint. A great bhakta of Rama, he was known to have lived like Hanuman for a long time, eating nuts and climbing trees. He was fond of bhajans and kirtans. When 'M' met him in his hut, he was thin and frail and very delicate looking. Crowning his ever-smiling face was a great chunk of wound-up matted hair and he smelled of Vibhuti. Taking a pinch of ash, he touched M's forehead with it, popped a couple of grapes into his mouth and said, 'Umm, needs to ripen, will ripen. Do bhajans'. 'M' meditated for a few minutes, prostrated and left the place.

Those days 'M' had a close Brahmin friend whose father worshipped Sai Baba of Shirdi. The moment 'M' saw Baba's picture, an irresistible desire to know about Baba's life rose in him. The next day Mr. Subramanya Iyer, an advocate, who was his friend's landlord, gave him a copy of the "Life of Sai Baba of Shirdi by Narasimha Swamiji." Then he lent 'M' Sai Sat Charita. He fell in love with the great Faqir.

At this time 'M' heard from a friend of his who was a medical student (he is now a neuro-surgeon) about a lady Avadhuta called Maayi Maa, who lived on the Kanyakumari beach. She was reputed to be over a hundred years old and no one could say where she came from or what language she spoke. The few words she said sounded very much like Bengali.

'M' went to see her alone. Kanyakumari is close to Trivandrum. He reached Kanyakumari around 1 P. M. He walked from the bus stand and came to the entrance of the Devi Temple. He casually walked across the rocky beach and there she was. A woman who looked to be in her sixties, she wore absolutely no clothes, her face a typically Bengali face, glowing, ageless eyes, smiling. She sat on one of the rocks with a circle of street dogs around her forming a security ring. The dogs snarled when they saw 'M'.

Maayi Maa scolded the dogs using peculiar sounds and they dispersed and sat at a distance. She motioned to 'M' to sit down. He sat down on a rock. She pointed to the bananas that he had with him and said something. He gave her the bananas. She fed the dogs some, ate two herself and returned a few to him. He closed his eyes and tried to tune in with her vibrations. After a long time he opened his eyes. She was still there. Giving a broad smile she said, "Jao, jao, thik..." The last word could not be made out.

When Paramahamsas say "Go", one has no business to stay, so 'M' prostrated and came away. After visiting the Vivekananda Rock, 'M' returned to Trivandrum.

He was made aware of the significance of Maayi Maa's darshan the following morning. Tired after meditating for a long time in the night, he could not bring himself to be up at dawn. As he slept deeply he had a wonderful and vivid dream. In the dream he was a mendicant with matted hair and wearing only a 'kaupin', sitting in padmasana and meditating under a Banyan tree which stood in the middle of a junction where four paths crossed each other. The jungle all around was thick.

A faint sound made him open his eyes, and from one of the paths he saw Maayi approaching with a stick in her hand. She was huge, much larger than life-size. Reaching the place where he sat she touched his chin and said, "Give me something to eat."

He told her, "Maayi Maa, I have only two grains of parched rice hidden in my matted hair."

She said, "Give me."

Without hesitation he gave the rice to her. She said to him, "Are you hungry?" He said "Yes, but you eat it Maa." She ate with great relish and turning to him said, "Your hunger is for a different thing. Close your eyes."

He closed his eyes. She pressed the middle of his forehead hard with what seemed to be her thumb. An ocean of bliss filled his whole being with its centre in the forehead. Every cell of his being was suffused with it. He lost his body consciousness. Only the other existed.

Then he woke up. The dream vanished, but O! How fortunate! The bliss remained. He was like a drunken man who had his fill. Slowly he sat up and stretched his legs and carefully went to the bathroom, afraid that he would fall. In a few minutes he got full control over his body and mind but the stream of bliss continued in the core of his being. It has since remained with him. At times low, at times high, but always there.

Already acquainted with the teaching of the Sufis by attending meetings of local Sufi groups and meeting some of the Amirs of the different Tariqats, he went at last to a gem among Sufis.

That was Kaladi Mastan who lived naked on the beach near Bimapalli in Trivandrum. He was drinking a cup of tea given by a follower when 'M' first saw him. He smiled and gave 'M' the rest of the tea. Then he said, "Big thief came to steal the treasure. Take it legitimately." Then he lit a cigarette and said 'smoke'. 'M' smoked. Then he took it back. 'M' sat and meditated before him. He covered M's head with sand and further cleared the conduits. He behaved like a mad man and many even thought he was mad, but he was a priceless gem and the few who were serious knew. He is physically no more now. Many visit his tomb.

Not very far from there lived Poontharasami, another God-intoxicated person with matted hair, who was mistaken by many to be a madman. When 'M' visited him, he suddenly stood up and kicked 'M' on his chest. That was a timely kick. It cleared the passage through which the mighty energy travels.

When 'M' went to thank him a month later, he had vanished, nobody knew where. An impressive looking fraud, who claimed to have been his closest disciple, tried to influence 'M'. The poor chap did not realize that 'M' could read him like an open book.

When he was twenty, 'M' made up his mind to go to the Himalayas. First he went to Madras by train, spent sometime in the Theosophical Society, then took a train to Delhi. From Delhi he went to Hardwar. From Hardwar he decided to walk.

All the money was finished. He had no intention of writing back home for help or even to let them know where he was. He knew he would be looked after, that the minimum needs of the body would be taken care of by the great powers that run the universe, and he was right. Of course, at certain times, he was tested thoroughly but in the end everything was fine. On foot he covered the entire journey from Rishikesh to Uttarkashi, to Gangotri, Yamunotri, from Batwari to Kedar via Buda Kedar, then to Badrinath.

At Rishikesh, he decided to stay in the Divine Life Society and continue his studies and meditation. It is a lovely place for sadhaks.

The Ganges flows nearby. Yoga is taught in the Ashram. The senior swamis are a great help and when one has time, one can wander around and meet sadhus of various sects. Satsang is most important for a sadhak.

That pilgrim-season found 'M' walking again to Badrinath – sometimes on the common pilgrim routes, sometimes through forests, staying in roadside dharmashala and chattis and many a time in forest hermitages beside the river. He gathered much food for the soul.

Reaching Badrinath after many days' journey, he first slept in the choultry. It was quite cold and his single blanket was insufficient, but he was in no mood to seek help. Those were the days when the fire of spirituality burned so bright that everything else, even the bare necessities – food, clothes and shelter – melted into insignificance. A highly intoxicating, ecstatic mood came over him in the great Himalayas. He attributed this, as also his intense sadhana to the presence of highly evolved beings in these regions. He hoped to meet some of them.

His physical difficulties were solved by the arrival of a Brahmachari whom he had met in the Divine Life Society. He was an experienced pilgrim who had travelled many times. Quickly he found 'M' an independent Kutir and persuaded him to stay there. He also got 'M' a couple of blankets and a wooden plank to sleep on; he also arranged with the Nepali Dharmashala for his food. He introduced 'M' to the Rawalji, the chief priest of Badrinath, and took him on a sort of conducted tour on most evenings.

In Badrinath as in other pilgrim centres, there were beggars wearing saffron, others wearing the holy robes to make a living, even sadhus who stole Kamandalus and blankets from each other.

Genuine yogis and paramahamsas also existed side by side, mingling with the common crowd and often deliberately pretending to be one of them.

Eager to see more of such souls and learning that they lived beyond Badrinath and on the other side of Narayan Parvat, 'M' decided to travel further. Without informing anyone, one morning he started off with his Kamadalu, staff and blanket.

He had earlier explored about a kilometer of that road on his previous visit to Badrinath but beyond that the territory was unknown. After about six or seven kilometres of not easy climbing, he reached the confluence of the Saraswati and the Alakananda, called Keshav Prayag. Close to this is the cave, which, an old sanyasin had once told him was the Vyasa Guha.

Beyond Vyasa Guha he could not proceed. Astrange force seemed to make his feet heavy. His heart overflowed with bliss but his legs would not move away from the cave. He took this as a signal and walked into the cave. Inside it was not as cold as it was outside. From there he could see the neighbouring snow-clad peaks. Spreading the blanket, he sat in Padmasan and went into a deep meditative state.

He must have sat in this state for a long time because when he opened his eyes it was evening and darkness was fast approaching. Right there before him was the same man whom he had met when he was a boy, but the evidence of whose guidance he had felt all through his life. He was more than father, mother or beloved and that instance he realised that he was his guide, his master.

He smiled, a very fair young man with long hair, almost beardless and what a smile it was! M's hair stood on end and he laughed, his eyes filled with tears.

"No place for hysterics," said the calm voice, this time in English. He stroked M's shoulders. Back in control 'M' touched his feet. He sat down near 'M' and right into the night and till dawn the next day the teachings and discussions went on. 'M' received all that he needed.

'M' spent three and a half years with his Master travelling all over the Himalayas. The Master advised him to go back to the plains and lead a normal life and begin teaching when commanded to do so. The Master promised to keep in touch. The Master had thoroughly overhauled his thought-process and brought about a lasting change in his consciousness.*

According to the Master's advice, 'M' went back to the plains, met many spiritual teachers and godmen, travelled all over India, took up difficult jobs to earn a living and "see the world at close quarters," as he put it. He also lived for a short while like a very materialistic minded person, and found that compared to the spiritual life and its greater vistas, the life of the worldly man is almost nothing. The joys of the spirit are much superior and it is the worldly man who renounces real happiness that springs from the heart.

But all that experience was necessary to tackle the worldly-wise who would say, "Oh! what do you know of the bliss of sensory experiences. You have not had any."

* The psychic channels in the spine and brain were opened up and the dormant energies activated so that the contact between the mind and the higher Consciousness was re-established.

Now 'M' feels that he can say with confidence, "Friend, I know, and there is nothing to go ga ga about."

Off and on he had attended the talks of J. Krishnamurti in Madras and elsewhere and read most of his literature. Finally he met him and had a forty-minutes' private discussion after which he decided to stay on in the Krishnamurti Foundation for sometime. The Master had said that Krishnamurti would be the last of the important persons that 'M' would meet as part of his education and had instructed him to pay particular attention to everything that 'K' did and how the organisation would function when he lived and after his death. 'M' had close contact with J. Krishnamurti during the last two years of his life and was made a Trustee of the Krishnamurti Foundation, which position he resigned after five years.

After K.'s death 'M' married Sunanda whom he had met in Vasant Vihar, the headquarters of the Krishnamurti Foundation, and became a householder. He now feels that no one can say to him, "Well, brother, it is alright for you to say, 'lead a spiritual life and live in the world etc., because you are unmarried...' and so on." 'M' lives with his wife and two children. "In fact, it is the best thing to do in this period of the earth's existence, for, Sanyasa is only for the rarest of the rare," says 'M'. With the blessings of his Himalayan Master and by strenuous Sadhana 'M' has transcended theories and scholarship and is established in higher consciousness.

The Master had said to 'M', "Do not advise people if you cannot follow the same advice. Do not talk on something if you have no personal experience." Wonderful teaching indeed! If only teachers follow this teaching what a lovely world this would be!

– Gp. Capt. (Retd.) Ratnakar Sanadi

1. THE OPENING

YES, GOD EXISTS! Whatever you like to call it. And if this sounds like some nonsense that intellectuals shun and fools (God bless them!) believe in, I say: "Hold on!"

Don't let intellectual arrogance destroy your being. Think carefully, for you are merely prejudiced. The believer in God is as prejudiced as the atheist for both affirm or deny without due enquiry. It would be better if you say: "Let me find out." Isn't that the correct attitude, the right approach?

Has this wonderful complex world come about by accident? Or, is there a Supreme Intelligence behind all these happenings, however difficult this may seem for our puny brains to discover its plans and motives?

On the other hand, do you think the world revealed to you through your sense organs is a real, solid, substantial one? Ask the physicist. He'll tell you: "It's all mere vibration; particles or charges in constant motion or just waves of different frequencies in a perpetual flux.

Your three-dimensional world is largely a concoction of your senses and mind."*

And you?

You are the consciousness which is the witness of all the drama, watching in amusement as the ego plays its games, dons different masks at different times and ends up identifying itself with the roles it plays. The real you is that ever-blissful, unchanging, blessed consciousness.

Therefore, enter. Enter the door that opens onto the path that seekers have trodden for thousands of years.

Abandon not the infinite ocean of bliss and happiness that knows no end but is itself the end of the road. Some call it 'God', some 'Truth', and some 'Nothingness', for it can't be described by words or gestures.

It is more precious than anything your mind can conceive of and O! how fortunate that this priceless pearl is not far away in some inaccessible part of the world or hidden in the dark bowels of the earth. It is nearer to you than your own jugular vein. It is Bliss Supreme which the sages of yore imbibed and which then made them dance in ecstasy. It is your very 'Self'.

Will you, ignoring this great treasure, play with mere trinkets? It is for this blissful being who shines through every heart that man searches everywhere except within.

* The imagination working on the data collected by the sense organs conjures up a world of fantasy which hypnotizes one. To realise the Truth is to de-hypnotize oneself.

Like the musk-deer that carries fragrant musk under its own tail and searches for the source of the fragrance all over the forest, under thorny shrubs and under dangerous snake holes, human beings likewise search endlessly for happiness mistaking pleasure – the short interval between sorrows – for the real thing.

But the blissful supreme is right here – so simple and clear. No one need shave his head or wear special headgear or ochre robes or run away from all that one holds dear. No Sir! You may live in this world and do your duties, earn your livelihood, look after those that need your help, spread the fragrance of love and service, and yet remember to keep in touch with your true Self, the spark from the great fire, the drop from the great ocean, by meditating regularly, so that, in the spotless clear mirror of your heart, Divinity's reflection glows. From your heart, then, will the serene rays of the spirit proceed and fill other hearts with bliss.

First, you may get what you want if you ask with all your heart, and then you will discover what you truly need and seek for it and it shall surely be granted. "Ask and it shall be given thee," said a great Master, "Seek and ye shall find. Knock and it shall be opened unto thee."

Of course, the master tests your patience. Therefore, knock persistently but wait patiently. Then will your heart be filled with supreme bliss and you will work for the good of mankind.

Sorrows and shortcomings, the cares of this world, are there certainly, but who doesn't have them? Now you, the traveller on the path should know that they are lessons for you, and that after each obstacle is overcome, the road becomes smoother and easier. And overcome you will. There is no doubt.

So let nothing stand between you and the overflowing cup of wine that lies so near and yet so far. Drain the cup and declare: "There is but One, the blissful Truth. Nothing else exists."

The master shall come to him who seeks the 'Truth' with all his heart. Of this have no doubt. It is the master who seeks the true seeker, not the other way around. So work and pray and meditate. Seek the kingdom of the spirit. The rest shall be given to you unasked.

"Step firmly upon the path. Have no fear.
Fearlessness is close to 'Truth'."

2. THE PATH

IS THERE A WAY to the bliss divine? Is there only one way or are there many? As many human beings exist in this world, so many ways exist, for there is no single magic formula or esoteric rite which will transform one instantaneously. Supreme perfection cannot be purchased off the bookshelf nor by bribing the guru or God. All those are tricks you use in everyday life. They don't apply to the Supreme Self. If someone promises salvation all at once, take care; you are about to be hoodwinked. If someone guarantees to lead you to Supreme Bliss in a certain number of days, again be on guard. No human being can ensure it; only the Divine knows.

So there are different paths depending on the kind of disciple, the kind of guru, the special circumstances and other external as well as internal factors. One teacher may be well-suited to a certain kind of disciple and ill-suited to another. The genuine teachers know this. Once in a thousand years or so appears a great Master who can lead one through all or any one of the paths. This is indeed a very rare occurrence.

However, there are certain essential factors of a spiritual journey and these apply to all paths.

1. The aspirant is sincere in his search.
2. He has understood (in theory) what he is looking for, or to put it in another way, knows what he is not looking for.
3. He is prepared to listen and learn without prejudice.
4. He is ready to swim against the stream.
5. He is prepared to practise regularly and diligently.
6. He is patient.

By saying that the aspirant is sincere, I mean that he is not pretending, for various reasons, to be a religious man. He is ready to speak the truth and learn the truth. He does not advertise his religious inclination by changing his robes or overestimating his capacity to renounce, run away somewhere, and cut himself off from his environment. Such actions have a whiff of hypocrisy, and in the end, confuse and confound one self and others too. True, the renunciant is a very highly evolved being but real renunciation is rare and is no joke.

Moreover, one may live in the world and not be stained by it. Such persons are needed today. May such aspirants increase in number! May noble thoughts come to us from every side!

Now, what is the sincere aspirant looking for? Why is he doing so? Aren't the pleasures of the senses enough for him, surrounded as he is by all the luxuries of the world?

Looking about him in all directions, while still playing his role in the drama of this world, the discriminating aspirant sees how fleeting the enjoyments of the world are. In his mad race towards the fulfilment of his desires, man does not pause to consider how pleasures are followed by pain, and how, whatever one achieves, one is still left with a feeling of want, the unending hunger and thirst, a covetousness that never ceases until death with its final blow makes null everything that has been held so dear and ends the race with total extinction. And death is not far away. It lives with us. Isn't death our constant companion? How terrible it would be if things don't die but last forever. It is because death destroys the old that it is made possible for the new to be born, and this process goes on and on. In fact, every second (or fraction of a second) the present dies and becomes the past for a new present to be born. So death is very much a part of life. Don't we die every day, every second, as the present moment turns into the past and becomes a dead thing only to be stored in the memory?

Ask the biologist and he'll tell you; millions of cells die every day, every minute, to be replaced by new ones. And yet when death strikes the individual, he is often caught unawares. No one knows when it comes and the human being likes to believe that it is far, far away.

Watching, observing all this carefully, he begins to wonder, what am I seeking? I seek joy, and sorrow raises its ugly head. I get hold of what I desire and then comes the fear of losing it, of somebody taking it away, or losing it when I die. I see the beautiful moon, and time, the great snatcher, snatches it away and I am left with an image I keep craving for, again and again.

I build and the nature destroys because it has its own building plans. Today's palace is tomorrow's random rubble. Where is the permanency I seek? Where is the real happiness, the supreme joy that I seek?

Says the master: "Agreed that you experience joy when coming into contact with the objects of the world. But the joy wells up in your own heart, doesn't it?"

Does the enjoyment take place in the object or in yourself? All joys spring forth from within your being, my dear friend. The reservoir of all joy, the essence of all bliss, is in your own heart, in the core of your own being.

The rishis, the mystics, the saints, have all found the way to tap the source of perennial joy within, without resorting to external objects.

This blissful fountain is your real 'Self', your real being. Search for it with your teacher's help. In fact, you are 'it' and when you discover this, you'll get an idea of what the Higher Self is.

This 'Self' of yours is ever free, ever blissful. It is and was never bound; therefore, there is no question of making it free. It is always free. It manifests itself as the 'I', the consciousness, the 'I' that exists eternally in the waking state, dream state, and deep sleep, the 'witness' of all states of consciousness. This is the real 'you', the blessed, blissful 'Self'. The mind, borrowing the 'I' from it, mistakenly feels bound and attempts to make itself free.

You are eternally free. You are existence-consciousnessbliss, unpolluted by anything that happens in the relative world. You are free. Shake off the illusion that you are bound and rejoice in absolute freedom and absolute bliss.

You don't need to do anything to be free when you are already free. So, relax and sit firmly and reflect on this truth until your mind settles down, the false movement of constant becoming ceases, and your 'Self' shines forth in all its glory, reflecting the majesty of the higher 'Self' – God.

But alas! The mind does not settle down so easily. Therefore, I shall give you a simple technique discovered by the ancient rishis. You don't have to escape to the caves to practise it. Practise in your own house, in the midst of your daily life. Practise three times a day or at least once.

Remember! There is no technique to reach the 'Truth', for you are yourself the 'Truth'. Techniques are there to still the mind so that it understands the truth that the mind cannot reach the 'Self' and settles down perfectly, so that the Self – the ever-blissful 'Self' – alone shines forth.

Now, begin to practise immediately and be free. Don't wait; for, every second you lose by postponing is a great loss indeed.

3. ABHYASA – THE PRACTICE

FIND A QUIET CORNER where you may sit calmly without being disturbed for at least ten minutes everyday, preferably twice, at dawn and dusk, or at least once a day. Ensure that there is enough ventilation to allow fresh, sweet breeze to enter.

This has its own advantages. The conducive vibrations of the place in which you practise build up as days go by until they are able to influence your mind the moment you sit down.

This is why many meditators prefer to use a small special room or shrine exclusively for the purpose of meditation. That is, of course, the best thing to do, but if you find it difficult to set apart a meditation room, you could use any quiet corner as I have mentioned above. Even your bed will do, but take care. Since a bed is meant for sleeping, the subtle influence of sleep may overpower you as soon as your mind begins to calm down and you may find yourself falling asleep. This has been the experience of many meditators except the most advanced who can even meditate in the market place.

It is also advisable to have a set of clean, loose-fitting and comfortable clothes which are to be used only for meditation.

Although the above are ideal conditions, you do not have to worry too much about the details as long as you can sit down in a quiet place, indoors or outdoors, undisturbed, and practise your meditation.

Wash your arms and face and feet before you sit in a comfortable posture on your seat. Face any direction you like but try to stick to the same direction everyday.

First of all, thank the Lord for the food and shelter you have been provided with. Then, if your window overlooks a river or a lake or a forest or a lovely garden, take a good look and observe the beauty of nature. Take a few deep breaths as if you are filling your lungs with the splendour and vitality of nature.

Then, broadcast your love to all of creation mentally and give special attention to those who are supposed to be your enemies. Think that you are filling your being with love with each inhalation and sharing it with others when you exhale.

Now, if you like, before you begin the actual practice, you may perform the usual prayers, rituals, etc., which have been taught to you before. Hindus can practise sandhya vandana, or simply chant the wonderful Gayatri Mantra a few times. Muslims may practise their

Namaz, an excellent spiritual exercise. Christians can chant their prayers which include the 'Sermon on the Mount': "Our Father who art in heaven...", Buddhists may chant "The Jewel in the Lotus", the Sikhs their Satnam, and so on.

After this is over, sit in a comfortable, relaxed and yet firm posture. Sukhasana or sitting cross-legged as one does while eating is fine, or if one has had enough training, Padmasana or lotus posture in which Buddha is usually depicted. Sitting on the heels with head bent and chin pressing the upper part of the chest in a chin-lock (bandha) as Muslims sit for prayer – the Egyptian posture – is also suitable. The main idea is to keep the backbone erect and yet not suffer pain or discomfort.

Those who cannot sit in any of these postures may sit on a cushion or chair. It is foolish to try to twist yourself into difficult postures without previous training. When there is pain, the mind gets distracted and will remain occupied with it and will refuse to ascend to higher things. So be comfortable but not so comfortable as to fall asleep.

Inhale deeply and consciously a few times. Relax! for, concentration and meditation come with relaxation, not with tension. Then begin to chant any of the well-known mantras you might have learnt. Om Namashivaya is good, so is Om Sri Ram Jai Ram or Hare Krishna or Allah-hu or merely hu or Om. The idea is that it should be concise, not long and unwieldy. If you so desire, I shall give you one mantra: 'So Hum' which means 'That I am'.

Now, the important thing is to combine your breathing with the chanting of the mantra. Don't chant audibly; chant mentally. When you inhale, chant 'So', and when you exhale, chant 'Hum'. Chant nine rounds, one inhalation and one exhalation making one round.

Then – this is most important – give up trying to control your breathing consciously. Instead, allow the inhalations and exhalations to follow their own rhythm. You merely watch the inhalation and exhalation quietly, meanwhile continuing to chant 'So Hum' mentally with each natural inhalation and exhalation.

Now, fix your mental gaze at a spot just below your physical heart or at the point between the eyebrows. Pinch once lightly any one of these spots you have chosen to help you fix your attention there. Visualise a silvery flame, cool and radiant like the moon, shining in your centre of attention. Or, you may visualise a lovely rose, a lotus, or a star. But stick to any one symbol and centre. Don't keep changing and shifting. Personally, I would suggest a blooming, radiant lotus in the heart-centre but leave it to you to decide.

As you watch your breath silently chanting 'So Hum', you will find that the rhythm of breathing slows down considerably and a certain peace and tranquility begins to emerge and envelope your whole being. Often, at this stage you feel like giving a deep sigh. The sigh denotes that your psyche is beginning to relax and settle down.

The great rishis discovered this secret of pranayama when they found that a calm, slow rhythm of breathing always accompanied a tranquil mind and a fast breathing pattern indicated tension and agitation. You can discover this for yourself if you observe your breathing and mind under various circumstances. This is true pranayama, not the forced holding of breath which could cause internal haemorrhage or worse.

As you calmly observe your breathing, and as the breathing pattern becomes so slow and soft that you can hardly feel it, stop even watching the breathing, and fix your attention only on the lotus that blooms in your heart. Abandon even the 'So Hum'. Just sit there, feeling the blissful presence of the Lord, who is bliss itself, filling your heart with the nectar of joy. You are yourself that joy.

As you practise daily (and with the master's help which is surely there) you'll enter subtler spheres of consciousness and bliss. You will see lights and hear heavenly music and witness wonders, but tarry not. These are merely signposts and sometimes temptations. Keep marching ahead quietly until you come face to face with the 'Presence', who is within and not far away.

At times, your breathing may even cease briefly. This is keval kumbhak but there is a greater keval kumbhak where there is cessation of all thoughts. There is no incoming thought or outgoing thought. There is only the 'One Pure Witness', unaffected Satchidananda, watching the drama.

Of course, in the beginning, thoughts will come, sometimes in torrents, but don't worry. Don't try to throw them out. Watch calmly as you would a mischievous child and they'll settle down and disappear.

Thoughts are like ripples that disturb the calm surface of the mind and distort the reflections. When they disappear, the surface becomes clean, and the undisturbed reflection of the 'Sacred One' is glimpsed, however briefly.

What is important is to understand that you are really the ever free, radiant, blissful being, and sit quietly. Everything else is irrelevant and cannot harm you in any way. "Meditate and discover this," said the rishis of yore.

When you get up from your daily meditations, thank everything and everybody with utter humility.

4. BENEFITS

WHAT BENEFITS does one derive from the practice of the technique discussed above? You will soon begin to experience a lightness of body and mind. You will be less tense, less agitated, and in the business of daily life, more efficient. Modern medicine has discovered that many physical ailments have their beginning in mental stress. You'll be saved from them on account of the relaxed condition of mind that you are able to induce daily. Since a tension-free mind can think more clearly and without confusion, you'll see that your thought processes begin to get into top form.

True, the dirt and rubbish that you have gathered in the past will at times come to the surface, but don't worry. That's how they are thrown out and got rid of.

You'll also begin to get a new feeling of unselfish love and compassion towards other living things. From the lower centres, the thrill will ascend to the heart centre above, and whenever you encounter a beautiful thing, be it a bright flower or a lovely peak, or an old solitary tree, your heart will thrill with divine bliss.

But all these things are, so to say, fringe benefits. The real goal is still not attained. Don't also mistake the technique for the goal. Go on meditating deeper and deeper until the mind is stripped bare and you find your own dear 'Self', the radiant unpolluted, indestructible, pure consciousness, the unalloyed bliss. May the master guide you in this supreme adventure.

5. ADJUNCTS

IS IT ENOUGH if one just meditates twice a day or five times a day? Not exactly. From times immemorial the sages and prophets have laid down what are called rules of conduct which a religious person should practise. While rituals and ceremonies may be dispensed with if found unnecessary and cumbersome, the rules of conduct have to be studied carefully and adopted as far as possible, because, by practising them, your capacity to meditate is enhanced.

Given below are the yamas, the dos, and the niyamas, the don'ts, common to all aspirants no matter what formal religion they belong to:

Do not steal.
Do not kill.
Do not lie.
Do not be violent.
Do not commit adultery.
Do not drink intoxicating potions.
Eat in moderation – do not overeat.

Pray or meditate daily, if possible, twice a day.

Treat your parents and teachers with respect.

Be kind to your neighbours.

Lead a simple life.

Do some service to other human beings.

You'll notice that all these precepts, if practised, are surely conducive to peace and tranquility. If you steal, you always have the fear that you will be caught some time or the other. How can such a mind be calm and meditative?

If you kill, you know that it is most likely that you will be killed by someone too. The whole culture of violence where enemies kill each other is merely the symptom of a disease which lies deep in each individual. The desire to kill is necessary to win the race, but then who pauses to ponder over the fact that all joy and fulfillment lie within the heart and not outside? The same blissful Self which is in you is in me and one has only to meditate and live in peace to contact it.

If you lie once, you'll probably have to lie again and again to protect the original lie, and so on it goes – a vicious circle. Soon you have spun a web of lies which you are afraid might be broken and further lies are woven to prevent this. Thereafter, you even begin to believe your own lies.

How can such persons have peace of mind? So, throw all these things overboard and lead a simple, transparent life full of peace and tranquility. The small inconveniences you may feel are nothing compared to what you gain.

Now adultery. You know, spiritual progress is linked to the ascension of the mind into subtler and higher states of consciousness, the grossest points of which consciousness functions as hunger and sex, perfectly legitimate needs of any human being except that we pay too much attention to sex because it affords the maximum enjoyment we can normally conceive of and for a split second even makes us forget ourselves.

As one approaches subtler spheres, the consciousness has to be shifted from the lower centre of sexual satisfaction to higher centres of spiritual satisfaction. This cannot be done if one's mind is always centred on sex-related activities. Therefore, the emphasis on moderation in sexual indulgence. The ideal person does not go around indulging in sex at all times under all circumstances and become a prey to venereal disease or AIDS or other physical and mental diseases, all in the name of freedom. He gradually gets rid of the obsession by sublimating his sexual energies to higher emotions which lift his consciousness to greater and higher states of existence. In the upper centres, like the heart centre, for instance, he enjoys a bliss that is a thousand times more powerful than mere sexual enjoyment. Therefore, the advanced yogi needs no sexual enjoyment in the usual sense of the term.

Such a person may or may not indulge in physical sex depending on various factors but can he ever be an adulterer?

Closely connected to sex is the question of food. The best way to control a wayward mind is an occasional fast. The yogi, a practitioner of spiritual exercises, needs to moderate all his activities in order to be able to progress in his endeavour. Mark you, moderation is the key word.

The Gita puts it succinctly: "This yoga is not for him who eats too much or too little, who sleeps too much or too little." That sums it up. While it is true that vegetarian food is indeed conducive to meditation, especially in the beginning, it is also true that vegetarian food can be made so rich and spicy as to cause lethargy – a sure obstacle to meditative states. There are also people who overeat and claim that it is all right as long as it is vegetarian food. Surely, overeating is a tamasic act, not a satvic.

Don't be obsessed with what you eat and what you don't – a trait which Swami Vivekananda called 'the religion of the kitchen'. Eat what is nutritious, what your body needs. Take medical advice if necessary but eat in moderation. If you see somebody eating food which you do not fancy, do not imagine that he is an ignorant person or a spiritually undeveloped one. Remember that Swami Vivekananda ate meat and the great saint Ramakrishna loved fish. Of course, this does not mean that you should eat fish or meat because they did. Use your common sense.

Vegetarianism by itself divorced from other factors may not be the sign of a saint. Hitler was a pure vegetarian. He did not even eat eggs, but was he a saint? How many thousands of Jews did he send to the gas chambers?

As far as intoxicants are concerned, one doesn't have to be extraordinarily intelligent to understand why one is advised to abstain from them. Anything that makes one unbalanced and lose one's sense of proportion and judgement has to be abandoned.

Your reasoning faculty is a very important instrument and an intoxicant destroys it gradually, apart from causing physical ailments and the curse of alcoholism or other forms of addiction. The habitual drinker or drug abuser overestimates his abilities and commits blunders. Many road accidents are the result of drunken driving. The false sense of euphoria and self-importance induced by alcohol or drugs is followed by depression. Ask the addict how he dreads his hangovers or cold turkeys and yet he waits eagerly for his next high. Addiction is slavery, mental and physical, be it alcohol or drugs. Drugs are, however, the more dangerous of the two since they can cause permanent damage to the brain.

"Okay," some may say, "are we to cut out all that we enjoy from our lives? If we don't drink occasionally how are we going to get away from the sorrows and cares of the world? We will become more frustrated, more violent. There is no other state of altered consciousness that we know of."

Now, wait a minute. You are not cutting out every joyful thing from your life. You are only exchanging lesser joys for the springs of joy that can well up within your heart. You will no longer complain when they begin to flow.

Also, there is something you could start drinking right away – a better substitute for your daily peg. The wondrous wine of chanting the name of God, singing for Him, in Him, about Him, pouring out your love to Him, playing musical instruments, dancing before Him: O! How sweet are the lovelorn songs of Meera, how heavenly the strains of her tampura. Sing and dance to your heart's content. Absorb yourself in devotional music and let it carry you to higher states of consciousness. Once you taste the wine of devotion, you'll never want to touch lesser intoxicants.

But let me caution you. Music must be pure. Full of devotion. It shouldn't degenerate into cheap entertainment. Also, it is only a means to an end. Don't forget that the aim is union with the Divine Lover, or as some others might put it 'sieving the ore to discover pure gold'.

Then the question of service. No one can meditate for twenty-four hours or remain engage in devotional activities. There are exceptions but we are talking of the general. Therefore, find sometime when you are neither engaged in earning your bread or in praying, to do whatever you can for your fellow human beings.

The only gods you can actually see with your physical eyes are these living gods. Serve them but remember while doing so to be thankful to them for providing you the opportunity to serve them and thereby speeding up your spiritual progress. It is you who should be thankful, not they. Feed one hungry man even once and see how much easier it is to contact the Divinity when you sit down for meditation that day.

Someone asked me the other day, "Sir, are we to practise all these moral precepts to perfection before we begin meditation?".

That, Sir, is next to impossible. No one has ever succeeded in becoming morally perfect before beginning to meditate. The fact is that meditation and practise of moral precepts complement each other. Begin to meditate today. Do not postpone it. Side by side with this, attempt to follow the yamas and niyamas to the best of your ability.

As you progress, you'll become more and more morally perfect and so also will your progress in meditation become better and better. This will go on until you reach your final goal. Till then, there are bound to be imperfections. So don't worry. Only when one has perfectly understood that all that exists is the 'Self', will selfishness be completely destroyed. Doesn't all immorality spring from selfishness? As you approach nearer and nearer the blissful Self, you will find no need to behave immorally. Until then, do your best. Conquer hate with love.

6. THE LOVER

WHILE ALL THESE INSTRUCTIONS apply to most people, there is one exception – the true bhakta, the lover. He or she is caught up in a cyclonic love affair as it were with the Lord, the eternal sweetheart, and no rules and regulations apply to such fortunate souls.

Meditation, diet, religious observances, customs and manners, duties and responsibilities, none of these matter to this being. He throws the whole world to the winds and pines away for the Lord. Separation from his Beloved is unbearable for him and he goes mad with longing. He is unaware of anything else. And when the Lord finally comes, he doesn't bow down to Him. They, the lover and the Beloved, are then locked in the embrace of divine love until they cannot be distinguished, one from the other.

But a word of caution. Do not try to imitate him. Also, guard yourself against imitations. The one sure sign of a true lover is the absence of selfishness. If anyone pretends to be one and you discover even a tinge of selfishness, keep away.

True lovers of God are rare and, wherever they are, a flood of spirituality sweeps through and many are benefited by it. And yet most of such lovers refuse to be masters or guides since they are most of the time caught up in their own world of divine love.

A few of them, after having passed through the stormy stage and attained the highest, bring their minds down to everyday consciousness in response to the Supreme Being's command so as to teach others. Such teachers are indeed the greatest and fortunate indeed are the disciple of such a one.

But, once more I must warn you. Some mentally unbalanced persons and lunatics may behave like bhaktas. So take care. Absence of wisdom and presence of selfishness and lust are sure signs of fake bhaktas and lunatics.

The rishi, the jnana yogi, and the raja yogi are of a different type. They are calm, collected and tranquil, and can often teach even without uttering a single word. Silently they guide and transmit the energy which cleanses your heart and clears the passage for the ascension of divine power which is the very essence of bliss.

7. THE MASTER

WHEN THE TIME IS RIPE, the master comes. You don't have to search for him in the Himalayas. He may be living next door but you may not know. Your ignorance and arrogance effectively help him to remain hidden.

If you are a sincere aspirant, if your only goal in life is to find your true 'Self', if you constantly meditate and pray for guidance, the master shall surely come – if so required.

You may or may not recognize him but he guides you silently. The true master is the Lord himself who takes on various forms to guide the devotee.

Test the master well before you accept him. If there is even a trace of lust or selfishness in him, he is not of the highest status. Test him thoroughly but have patience. Do not judge in haste, for, many a time the actions of a master have been misunderstood. Mysterious are his ways. Do not judge his actions without finding out the motives.

Once you have decided after careful reflection, treat him with the greatest respect and beg of him to accept you as a disciple. You are fortunate if he does, because a true master is not fond of collecting hundreds of disciples. Rarely does he agree to be the guru.

A guide is necessary in almost all cases because you are starting on a voyage through a largely uncharted territory. You may find here and there greatly advanced spiritual beings who do not seem to have had a guide. They are exceptions, and though they may not have a guide in human form, understand that God himself guides them and looks after their needs.

Don't imitate them, for they belong to a special category. Do not even imitate your own teacher for you are not he. Follow his teachings and instructions instead and you'll bloom into a master in your own original way and not turn out to be a faint imitation; a shadow of the original.

A master may be young, old, male, female, fair or dark. The externals do not matter at all. What matters is his inner spiritual status. He may, if he so decides, help you wipe your heart clear of all the accumulated vasanas and make you free.

May such a master guide you!

DHYANA – MEDITATION
An Invitation to Bliss

"Knowledge merely acquired through books, in fact all theoretical knowledge, while it has its place, is not of much use unless proved by direct experience and realization"

"It is through direct realization that the inner core can be reached and the outer shell discarded."

"Dhyana – meditation – is the way to this inner realization and should be learnt personally from a competent teacher" – 'M'

According to 'M', there cannot be a general formula common to all. Each person has to learn the technique best suited to him after discovering with the help of the teacher, which method is best for him, depending on his physical and psychological characteristics and past conditioning.

For instance, one might require a Shiva mantra while another, a Vishnu Mantra, while yet another a Sufi name of God. And again one may be inclined towards Bhakti and another towards Raja Yoga and so on.

This requires personal contact with the teacher. A teacher may also be to speed up spiritual progress.

'M' initiates aspirants into spiritual practice after personal interview.

THE SATSANG FOUNDATION

"When you serve a less fortunate person in any way, material or spiritual, you are not doing him a favour. In fact, he who receives your help does you a favour by accepting what you give, and thereby helps you to evolve and move closer to the *Divine, Blissful Being* who in reality is within you and in the hearts of all beings."

This is the mission of Sri Mumtaz Ali, the founder of The Satsang Foundation and a teacher who spreads the message of the Vedanta.

True to its meaning, The Satsang Foundation is a coming together of people in search of truth, under the guidance of a teacher.

Thus, Sri Mumtaz Ali shares his spiritual experience with all those interested, holds talks and discussions on the Vedanta, teaches meditation and yoga for health, peace and tranquility, and encourages works of charity. In doing so, he helps people onward on their spiritual journey.

You may use the following address for further details and contacting Sri M:

Satsang Foundation
No.9 Webster Road, Cox Town,
Bangalore 560005.
Email: satsangoffice@gmail.com

Approach someone who has realized the purpose of Life and question him with reverence and devotion; he will instruct you in this wisdom. Once you attain it, you will never be deluded. You will see all creatures in the Self, and all in Me.

– Bhagavad Gita 4.34-35

Samvo manãmsi jãnatam

With our minds put together, may we understand.

Other Titles by Sri M

Wisdom of the Rishis:
The Three Upanishads: Ishavasya - Kena - Mandukya

Jewel in the Lotus: Deeper Aspects of Hinduism

How to Levitate and Other Secrets of Magic

The Upanishads - Katha, Prashna, Mundaka

Shunya: A Novel

On Meditation - Finding infinite Bliss & Power Within

The Journey Continues -
Sequel to Apprenticed to a Himalayan Master

Apprenticed to a Himalayan Master
A Yogi's Autobiography

The Autobiography of Sri M available in the following languages:
Hindi, Marathi, Tamil, Telugu, Kannada, Malayalam, Oriya, German, Russia, Bengali, Gujarati, Italian, Spanish, Japanese

The Journey Continues available in the following languages:
Hindi, Marathi, Gujarati, Kannada, Malayalam

9 788195 608980

Printed at Repro India Ltd.